SECOND SESSION:
AUDIO THERAPY II

PREFACE

My mom used to tell me, "The easier you get disappointed by things that happen to you, the more it will have a detrimental effect on you later in life. Take one day at a time and everything will work itself out."

SECOND SESSION : AUDIO THERAPY II

Second Session:
Audio Therapy Part II

Reggie Johnson

Events over the last few months have had my mind visualize myself knocking on a therapist door on a return visit. He tells me to have a seat and I plop myself on the couch. Pushing his glasses up and opening his book to take notes, he opens his mouth to say "Welcome back. What brings you back in for another session?" I take a deep sigh and just let it all spew...

TRAUMA

Breaking down
And I'm wondering who watching
Hmmm
I'm wondering who plotting
Hanging around in the background
Planting they seeds
who rotten

Now I feel dirty
Who mopping
While I had people window shopping
People think they 50 Cent
When I didn't even need they 2 cent
And that's on first 48

Don't need a detective
For this introspective
Not a stain on me
But I care to share some expletives

Fuck this
Fuck the trauma
And I put that on my own
My family's especially my mama's
Fuck the depression
Fuck the stressing
Fuck all the teachings
I been done learning the lessons

I just want to live
My mind my business
But God is my witness
People have they intentions

And they might sometimes be cruel
They don't know I burn rubber
And they just adding to my fuel

And just like that WB show
You ain't trying to see me in a duel
My eyes may be red
But I'm a blue dragon when I rule

I'm a king when I sit on my throne
Don't leave me and thoughts sometimes alone
Sometimes I wish I was still young
Done being grown
Enjoy this life while I can
I can't take this shit when I'm gone

FRAUD

Broken...
Closed off to everyone
But someone they had me open
Open, open up
Didn't see any magic but somehow
Open sesame
Came home to that apartment
And I felt like someone was messing with me
Expectancy
Life went down
When I felt myself
Crash into the ground
When suddenly my things grew feet
And gone without a sound
Nowhere to be found
Paint the red nose on me
I didn't know I had the makeup of a clown
But talk to me
Talk to me
I hold my hand out
Watch it take me to that little kid
Would tell my mom school was ok
Each day of school at times felt like a 10-year bid
She knew it
I was treated like a punk
Only thing that kept me going was school
As I made sure I didn't flunk
Swimming with the sharks
No trunks
No paddle

Like a fish out of water
Flashback to reality
And at times I think why bother
Why they feel like they can do that to me?
Why they make me feel so less then?
Is that what they want to see?
They wanted to see me
Crying real tears
How could they do this to me?

Who am I if they see I'm not perfect?
Who am I if they see me uneasy?
How long I'm an experience this feeling?
How I keep smiling and make it look easy?
Never stopped to look sleazy
Look at my legacy
And I say my family need me
Never thought I was a fraud
No, that cannot be me

CIRCUS

Over 31 days since I felt sane
It's like a leech has inhabited my brain
Sapping what used to be old me
And I depreciate into an imaginary story
Building up these blocks
and they reach a ceiling game over like Tetris
And getting claustrophobic, I need an exit

Looking at a clone version of myself
What is this duality?
Heartless regardless of what you find in me
Darkness spilled out looking for a key blade
Until then I sip some Dusse until I catch a fade
And don't think y'all can be slick and won't catch a fade
I won't think twice
No more Mr. Nice
Look back and say my night is made

31 days feels like I'm in a circus
Tightrope through this anxiety
Got me nervous
Hope those decrepit did themselves a service
Because you will never make me feel that I'm worthless

After letting all that out, the therapist can tell something was really bothering me. He stopped writing to look up at me and follows up with the question "How did all of that make you feel?"

UNHINGED

I did it
I became unhinged
Now that you watched it all unfold
I got you binged
People took some shots
And I got them by the syringe
This that part of the story when you begin to cringe

This about the time that you saw another side of me
Faded to black and it wasn't Jay Z that guided me
Never did I thought that I would have this inside me
Knowing what you seek, and I believe you want to hide from me

We not enemies.
We not friends.
This ain't make believe.
We don't pretend.

See the grin
We don't play kind to anyone
This ain't kindergarten
Or you guarding all your feelings
But this not show and tell
Arrested by my movements
And there's no bail
Demons inhabit my habitat
And they try to prevail
Let's see which outweigh the other
Bring your scale

I'm a chameleon
Not a vegan
Carnivorous
Because I'm eating
Every wordplay
Metaphor, simile
Who needs seasoning?
Writer's block?
That season's end
You thought it was the beginning of the end?

Yeah, think again

FUCK EVERYTHING

Hmmmm
Let me say this right quick
You couldn't see a draft from me
Even if I was the number one pick
Pulling thoughts out your ass
Like magic you a trick
Like magic you a Laker
Far from real you a faker
I should say you a risk
When I'm the risk taker
Screensaver
Sleeping until you have a task
Shutting down like a computer and crash
Never see another like me
Don't even try and ask
Don't even try and copy
What I say?
I hope you copy
No one will mimic
I am my own critic
No one could ever be this eccentric
Fuck em
Fuck em
Fuck em
Fuck em
Being angry becomes a chore
Looking for my product like a store
Just know that it's coming
Keep you coming back for more

You so pressed
Even an iron couldn't wrinkle you out
Caking ain't the word for it
Shit not sweet with your B.S. sprinkled
Throughout its just absurd for it
To be the only thing on your mind
It's criminal how minimal your actions
Do you remember the time
I gave a fuck about you?
Guess you made it through your 90 days
Fuck em
Fuck em
Fuck em
I'm still thinking this is all a phase

FLESH

It's been a while
5280 feet
It's been a mile
Running through these
Clips in my mind
That I can compile
All the time that I did smile

Right now
It's been a while
I look at myself and I feel the bile
I feel the sickness
Fill my body
It's been vile

Wearing my body
Like clothes
Swearing this that new style
Last time I saw you happy
It's been awhile

30 days to be exact
My body may be in the flesh
But my psyche still no
My mind from the soul
It detached
The devil took it
And won't give it back

OASIS

Bury my problems in a bottle with a pen
Getting closer to God
Although I surround myself with sin
People waiting for the losses
Never expecting me to win
People stuck close to me for comfort
At times I don't get that from my kin
Got your head gassed
Let me lighten with a pin
And then you'll complain I made you do it
At this point I'll look at you with a grin

Been in my little oasis
This year had a whole lotta changes
Nothing like my little oasis
Got to say life been amazing
Nothing like my little oasis
I love telling my mama I made it
Ain't nobody ever will change it
Living in my little oasis

Don't get me wrong
I had things go off course
Just kept thinking everything that happen
It could've been much worse
The words schooling me on how to cope
I couldn't listen to others discourse
If heavy is the head
The mind is an unstoppable force

24

Me and my thoughts
Going round for round
Yeah it's time to go fight night
Putting these what ifs to bed
It's time to go night night
If you scared of the dark
Just say so
Let me supply the night light
If I had to recount last 24
Hmmm, I got an idea
I called that a light bright

Let's go back 24 weeks
When all my memories
Felt I couldn't peak
Let's go back to those
That robbed my psyche and things
And they did it in a week
Ripped out and stomped on my soul
Strolling on my misery as if they were Greek

Switch gears and say Opa
Wish I could get them to the Greek
Look at em straight in they face
And see if things sweet when we speak
Keep playing if they want to with me
I ain't the one to let things leak
I ain't the one to let things slide
Ain't no games here on my playground
For weeks I felt like I was lost
Only till recently, I can say that I was found

May seem different
Like a startup, this toy been unwound
People go high too much
They don't dare to be mad and stay ground
Forever remain unbothered
But I'll be vicious like a bloodhound

24

24
Me and you got the same 24
Time moves different now
And only I know what it's hitting for
My therapy
Is the only reason this written for
I swear this shit is easy as sin
No reason it'll be forbidden for
Me
Who going to censor me?
Whose it going to be?
What would you do?
Yeah I'm listening...

The doctor noticed the strong feelings that depicted my mind and wanted to learn more. "And so how did it affect your relationships with family, friends and how you dealt with that invasion of privacy?"

MINDLESS (UH HUH)

Mindless...
Behavior that I'm trying to get right
No Mrs.
No teens from the 2000s
Going to make me see the light
No teens from the 1980s
Can tell me that I have seen stranger things
I been in this world for too long
Ain't no surprise what each day brings
I thank God everyday that He choose me
Because some days are good
Some days are bad
Still want to know He got me

Uh huh
No boys of the millennium
Although I went solo being unbothered
Seeing green got you so envious
When I see green I'll take them collard
When I see green I'll take it wired
When I see green, it's better not expired
When I see red
I'm left for dead
I'm a set everything on fire

Don't you second guess
Better not let my words get past you
Sidewalk chalk looking more permanent
traded it's ink when it went to tattoo
And are you up, are you down?
Arrested in your feelings

Have you lied down on the ground?

Uh huh
Mindless...
Timeless...

RAMBLINGS (WHAT YOU MEAN?)

Fuck it...
Fuck it...
Fuck this beat

Fuck this cadence
Fuck this wordplay
Fuck this laments...terms
I'm a read you like a book...worms
Eat it up
Defecate...worms
I just be dancing on the paper...worms

I'm too old school
For the new school
I just ride my own wave
Use the same hands to greet you
Yeah I make my own waves
And I suggest you act accordingly
Yeah that's right I need you to behave

Never beef
Never sides
I present myself respectfully
Check the slides
I just do it on my Nike
Check the slides
Besides...
I seek out competition
They like to hide
I'm a lion among them lying
Where's your pride?

Come outside...
Come outside...
You ok with who you are on the inside?
Don't run and hide
Don't confide
I'm at the destination you want to be
You want a ride?

Nah y'all don't
Nah y'all not ready
I just keep it old school
I rock steady
Don't be jelly
Don't be jelly
Nahs y'all full of it
Word to Belly

So, fuck it
Fuck this beat
What you mean?
Lately I been writing a lot
Feeling mean
Lately demons been hiding out
Now they seen
Now it's time to see what they mean

CHANGED

Been a stranger
I noticed shit changed
I'm different
I don't care the same
Some people say that I'm acting brand new
I'm on my HVAC
I'm keeping my cool
Running laps in your mind
We in two different pools
And I'm just learning how it was
To a degree we in different schools

Just know that I passed
Just know that this feeling going to last
Lot of people in my space like to dine and dash
Feed off my energy and leave when I crash
Feeding off me like the wanting some cash
Taking me out like I'm some of the trash
Fast off the break
Browned out like a hash

Been a stranger
I feel that shit changed
Now I feel like I'm crazy and deranged
Some people say that I'm adding brand new
Stirring it up like I'm brewing a stew
Coming back for seconds
I'm a give you a few
Cooking all the competition
Just preparing a roux
Just know I'm done with your games

No need to guess who
No need to ask names
Dragging me down
Like a horse to get maimed
Over the course of the year, I been mentally drained
Couldn't spill ink
The paper just stained
And my heart, that pained
Return harder than ever
The blade that slain
That stand in my day
From yester to today
No longer will clouds
Hover over that are gray
Clocking all the comments
So, I got time today

SILENT GHOSTING

It's infectious how quick I can leech onto
Someone or something
The sensation that it brings
And when I look in retrospect
I see what I'm doing, and it stings
Wake up, wake up
Hey, snap out of it
Quit digging yourself deeper
Going to make it hard to get out of it

Maybe I don't want to leave this feeling
In some instances, I care less
And sustain it all as a healing
And majority of the time
I fold based on these cards they were dealing

It can be friends, fabricated crushes
Anyone with common interests
Created a realm of happiness
Where repercussion is senseless
An attachment too significant
Be too good to be true
And I have to step away
To not lose that feeling of something new

It could take days
It could take weeks
For us to hang
Or even speak
I just know when it reaches months
Then I know the bond was at its peak

Maybe I was afraid of losing it
So that's why now we less frequently speak
Or I continue to self-deprecate
And envelope the feeling of being weak

And when that happens
I go Casper
I can be friendly
I now just like to ghost
Maybe it's routine now
When I feel myself doing the most

SLIMEBALL

Tired
Trumped you into thinking you was the business
You're fired
Inspired...
A lot of words
Lot of sentences
Lot of poetry
Dusse cognac is the drink of choice they pour me
Enriched in being against me
What a piss poor enemy
A century...
It would've taken a 1000 years
Just for you to be 10% with me
And we never was 80/20
Couldn't create a single fraction
Couldn't capture a caption
No post no venues
But you were just an attraction to me
Didn't pay that much monetarily
But my heart paid the heartache
Now I'm up here writing in the spirit
A la Drake
It took years to get good as this shit
If you would've stayed with me
It would've been as good as it gets
I would've bet on the spread then for us to split
Been around the world so many times
But you were always a trip
Thought I saw a New Year, New You in January
February, you took my heart for a minute

And for a few weeks I thought I hit my luck
Marching through the spring of books
April May be the time I see things warm up
June I see you blow off a little steam
July you want independence
Want the fireworks and streams
August you continue to be hot headed
Can't handle you mean
September caught us dancing
By October we were romancing
November you want for us to be cool
But December you want second chances

As I stopped and watched him continue to write notes down in his notebook, I was becoming more and more anxious. He stops for a moment and looks up at me and switches gears abruptly asking, "Now tell me about your childhood..."

YOUNG & NAIVE (USED TO BE)

I see glimpses of a young boy
With his Power Ranger toys
Cartoons and cereal
Racing to get homework done
Got to be number one
Then I go out and have some fun
Life felt so surreal

I remember those days
The ones that I didn't get my way
There goes my happy meal

Who knew that was metaphoric
To something that'd play out all my life
Every time I'm disappointed
It's like someone took a knife
Felt it with all its might
And now I feel like a low life

My mom used to say take it easy
My mom would say don't worry son
The sun rise and sets still
You don't get it now you're just young

Don't be so hard on yourself
Just live life and have some fun
Don't worry I got you my child now
Damn I was such a naive little one

Sitting here crying
Used to think I was dying
Because of reasons so dumb
She'd say you're disappointed now
Just think of what's to come

Words would haunt me through the sands of time
Become quicksand at the drop of dime
Don't lose me in the hourglass
Reach for my hand when I'm sinking
When I feel I'm overthinking
Reach for me with one last grasp

Thoughts linger from time to time
Like photos
And I shoot them down the best I can
As I see the young and naive little boy
I remember I became a better man

WHEN WE WERE YOUNG

Sundial keeps slowing turning
In the sands of time
Seems like nowadays I lose my sense
At the drop of a dime
Bring me simple
Craving the simplicity
Remember the good days
When there was only could
And not couldn't be
When it was ok to go out and play
And whether I would or wouldn't be

The simple things
And not the complexities
As I fight through the hardships
And some of them are scaring me
Don't like getting older
Moments are such a rarity

Now all we look forward to
Is internal peace and clarity

NOT FAR FROM HOME

I remember
In that Explorer, that's a Ford
Pen and notebook I could afford
Mama said when you get bored
Sit with your thoughts and record
And it was all she wrote

I remember
That night in third grade
I didn't get booed or berate
Who was controlling me at the mic
Feels like in the end I got played
And it was all she wrote

I remember
It was 2013
IG new on the scene
Had a following
It was serene
And it was all she wrote
I don't give a fuck
If you don't remember
I'm a winner
I'm a winner
Where's my fucking chicken dinner?
If you not at this table
You didn't put in summers and winters
Swear I'm not a saint
Been in rooms full of sinners
I rather keep a little fat
Than watch my pockets get thinner

I rather keep a few friends
Than a bunch of yes men
If I wanted to cause a storm
I would've joined the X-men
Class of 2012 Muskie
Yeah I joined the X-men
2014 became a best man
Ladies have Diggs me
and that's word to Taye
Been part of a game
And that's okay
Had to go through it
Just to know about ghosting
Now I'm quiet about it
Sorry if you chosen
Heart turned cold
My mind been frozen
So let go of all of the what if's
Don't keep it going
Not far away from home

"What's something that you've learned from all of these events the past few months?" This question stuck with me for a moment as I had to dig deep and ponder on it.

A LOT TO BE SAID

Hmph, damn...
A lot to be said
I'll take another trip instead
So much stuff going on in my head
Fuck them scars
I just let it all bled

Excuse me, I let it all bleed
So many people want me to succeed
So many people need to take heed
Live life without wants and only what you need
Like I only want for you mind your business
I want them to stop asking why I'm kid-less
I want addition, no need to deal with differences
I need no limits, where we go it is limitless

I'm one of a kind
And this is not poker
Weather you like or not
You're name not Al Roker
Stock up on my style
Better invest like you a broker
And I might say a few words for you
Like I'm a toaster

And watch me stack bread, right out the toaster
Celebrate all time, yet I'm not a boaster
Think you come close, you can be closer

THE OLD ME

I pray that this dies before it's too late
Been on thin ice for too long it's time to skate
Maybe it was meant to be, maybe it's fate
No, I'm not taking that, not taking the bait

Get hooked on someone else
Wasting your time going fishing
Saying that my help was wanted
Better check the listing
I know I am what
My heart been missing
Stop looking for myself in someone else
And just listen

I pray that the old me dies before you play me
Presented yourself that you was one that was here to save me
Now I'm sorry I could care less
And it was you that had forgave me
I wish it was nice to meet you
But what have you done for me lately?

METAMORPHOSIS

Like a caterpillar
Watch my metamorphosis
People cater to this pillar
Brits saying, they take a piss
At the fact I'm a pillar
Cater me with asparagus and fish
Because my food for thought
Is something I can dish

Better have an appetite
Or I'll leave your Adams apple tight
Choking hazard
Because many people try to bite
My style so ever changing
Every six months I'm saving the day's light
The day's light
I don't see any competition
Fall back or lose hours wondering
Wondering what you can bring in addition
Wondering what's new
But in a group you can't be any edition
Go solo Bobby Brown
My prerogative been winning

I'm on another wavelength
I'm just surfing
I'm a self sufficient
Young man
God fearing
Self-serving
All these thoughts in my mind
Be unnerving

Things I been through
No one is deserving
Got to go through what I go through
Yeah like my words I been verbing
No you in a different space then me
This noun be all reserve and
Playful with my banter
Really just good with all my wording
And don't let me get to the point
When I choose to get a word in

GRAVEYARD

All skulls and bones up in the closet
Yeah I'm on one so turn me off it
Or phlegm up what I think of you
Watch I cough it
My mind gone Waldo
Yeah I lost it
You lost yours when you violated my privacy
Illegally downloaded unstable thoughts
Committed piracy
I'm alive on this wire
Green and yellow don't bring a virus
Green and yellow going to pack a Lambeau up
Let's get high sis
High sis
I'm getting high sis
For two weeks
Went through an existential crisis
Couldn't tell everyone
Didn't want to feel lifeless
By bringing unwanted thoughts terrorizing my head
Like Isis
Ice is
Cooling me down
I let off too much heat
Just like the wants me to
But I won't accept defeat
We not playing on the same turf
Time to get you some new cleats
That artificial shit I'm used to
I got you beat
I might be a suburban motherfucker

Don't get me wrong I can assimilate to street
Decimate the greet
Tings, we past salutations
Don't need pats on the back or your congratulations
You made a breakthrough
For the record
I don't need a nomination
I dealt with so much
Pain and degradation
That just me speaking my truths
Is all the validation
You stole parts of me
But I'm a get my lick back
Reaper vibes are grim
I hope you don't sit and kick back

SECOND SESSION : AUDIO THERAPY II

"It takes a strong person to open up in a therapeutic way about personal instances that occur in one's life. And you obviously have not let that stop you. Going forward, what is your mindset and outlook on life persevering through trials and tribulations?"

A MORNING IN INDY

Even with a chest cold
I still want you to apply the pressure
Some of you entertain for 30 mins
Putting on a show being extra
Meanwhile my words run smooth
Wordplay riding a Vespa
Just wait for the stranger things to come
Alter ego is Vecna
Ain't no running up that hill
When the hills have eyes
I have a time with these timestamp songs
They just come to you as a surprise

And these words will live on forever
Nothing in ink will ever die
Even when we fade to black
Never leave you wondering why

But until then I got questions
How I got so many verses
And not too many sessions?
How I got so many verses
And they're not worshiped as the Bible?
I preach that I'm really him
And that's not me being prideful
Towering over my competition
Paris isn't it Eiffel
And I'm bringing you classics in the morning
Like coffee I'm internationally delightful

Stories you toyed with
Still take years to make a buzz

Under arrest by the pen
Never given to the fuzz
People wishing what really is
Or what really was
And I'm just over here watching it all happen
Just because

I like taking time off
Seems like I'm overwatched
And when I come back
Never will these words be botch
When they say it's time to turn it up
I said let me go grab a notch
And watch my shit age with time
Hmmm I'm a have to start drinking scotch

RAISE THE STAKES

Let's raise the stakes
Asparagus and mash
Accompany the plate
Only real ones sit at the table
Don't come in my circle
If you not willing and able

No fables
Only around me
Is people speaking the truth
If you ain't my babe
We ain't hitting it off Ruth
We ain't running no bases
If you ain't calling my phone
We ain't sliding nowhere if you stay at home

I raise the bar
100 grand like the candy
I like my vacations on a beach and it's sandy
Why settle for less
When you can have more like Mandy

I keep it current
The way I flow
Yeah sure is wavy
Thankful for
What the good lord gave me
Never the same
I can't be lazy

When I come for it
Y'all know better

No one that go better
Only one
Trendsetter
Go work for it
Do better

FEAR

Let's keep it real
Let's keep it a buck
Can you make a mil walk?
Or when you take shots
It's up and it's stuck

You miss 100% shots you don't take
and it's even more since I do this for sport
And this ain't my first take
This ain't Shannon Sharpe
Stephen A
Might keep it 513
Yet I still got fam in the A
Oh yeah
I got time today
Chuckie around you Rugrats
And in the night, this child's play
Yeah, I got time today
Been through too much recently
Got me feeling some type of way

That's word I'm a rich homie
Might be social but don't troll me
Might be a kid at heart but don't troll me
Might be italicized, you'll never get the bold me
Never say you miss the old me
Because you don't have to worry
Just wait for my next drop
It'll be here in a hurry

NEVER COUNT ME OUT

In my mind
I hear a ref counting down from ten
Round and round
Them birds will spin
As I think about what I have to lose
For the people that don't want me to win
And now I'm subjected to sin
Drink here, drink there
I just don't want just one instance
To leave a scare
Minus the e
I don't need that carrying a weight on me
Only things I carry the ink that was bottled up
For too long
Like I was stocking up in bulk
Like I'm in a crisis
I was there
I don't like this
My happiness
I did miss
Slowly coming back
A true bliss
And with every word
I write
I look back and reminisce
You took that from me
A sense of security
Karma coming for you don't worry
Don't wish harm on no one
But sometimes, it gets blurry
God going to handle them when the time come

DUMB ASSES

Quiet down...
Let me speak...
Me vs me...
No others compete...
Go ahead and get mad...
Grit your teeth
Always #1 priority
Others underneath...

Got a lot of things to be happy about
Got my people that bought in
While others wanted out
My own lane I'm always in
While others swerving out
Many want to pitch in
But they three strikes been out

And there goes the inning
Always going to get to the end
Ya'll wasn't there in the beginning
I'm just here to speak my truths
Others lie on here like linens
Only time I lie my head
Is when I count my winnings

I'm just a writer man
Cast away on another land
Man devise a plan
But end up trash can
Writer man
Who's a rider man?
Who's going to be there when it's rough?

Who's a rider man?
Who's just there for show and tell?
Who's an insider man?

Man damn
Writer man
I'm a writer man
If you don't give a fuck
I don't really give a damn
I'm a writer man
I'm a writer man

So shutcho dumb asses up

TROUBLED WATERS

I know one thing's for shore
That I been waiting and wading
Through troubled waters
Adversity became buoys
Making success become harder and harder
No matter I keep going
Where I come from gets farther and father
And to those that got something to say to me
I just think to myself why bother?

Why should I stoop to the same level
Of kids that never left the stoop kid
The votes been out on your character
And we didn't even all bid
You get a high of trying to make me feel low
And just to let you know it's been all mid
If you think I'm seeking resolution saying your name
I'm not, but God did

And God will watch over me
And then deal with you
Been very introspective
Looking at things from both point of views
I hear a lot of things they say
And some of them might be true
If I dropped to your level
And decided to meddle
But I ain't gassing nobody
I took my foot off the pedal

And put my foot on your neck
With my actions

Just watch this get traction
I use Drake as an inspiration
But these words are just a distraction
Don't worry I could if I wanted to
Fill up the socials with quotable captions
But I decide to put my all on to these
Just to get a reaction

I LOVE IT

I love it when my life content
Through action and intent
At that point
I can bring you content
Leave my legacy
And an imprint
And so far
It's just a dent

Ya'll going to pay for living in my head
This ain't free where's my rent
No, I didn't give my consent
Yet ya'll not going to violate
Took a cheap shot at my core
And stole a part of me
Had me irate
Now I make sure that my psyche don't break
Check once, check twice
Keep going until I'm locked in
I'm reinvested in my mental
So, you know where I got my stock in

I love it when I feel okay
I love it when the color permeates
Through this dark world full of
Black, white and gray
I love it when my life doesn't feel like it's disarray
I'll love it when my family straight
I love my mom with all my heart until it breaks
I love it when my brother dedicates to do whatever it takes
I love my grandma so much
I wish for her good health each day when I wake

I love it that I'm learning to love myself
I love it that you think taking a few hit points
That I'm down on my health
And just for constellation
I got a few things under my belt
Redirect that energy from all the pain that felt

GLAD YOU CALLED ME

Lately you have seen me lose it
You witnessed and watched me go through it
And repeatedly you say you can do it
Do it...
Just do it...
Says it so many times I'm going to need some more Nike's
Need that constant stimulation
Your words even excite me
I don't want anyone to come close
Don't think anyone could be

Sometimes I been a mess
And had to come clean
You've become a constant
A sure thing
No Miguel
But you're out of this world
My kaleidoscope dream
Can't wait to go to sleep each night
Without you nothing is as it seems

I live for your rhythm
With you I should never have blues
My heart at rest when we lay out and snooze
Tantalizing by nature
Yet hip hop being so naughty
Whenever you say my name
I'm so glad you called me

FPS

First person shooter
Hope you can see my point of view
People be bored playing games
And still seemed to don't have a clue
May seem like this poetry getting old
And I still treat it like it's something new
Never be a false positive
When you test me, I swear it's true
That I can hold my own against anyone
And that ain't nothing new

We can do single or go campaign
My words may seem to seek and destroy
Don't worry I just detain
Many people sit on the sides and complain
Try and come spar with me
You going to have to come train

I been doing this for the same years
As the coin that has Washington
Rinse, cycle, repeat
You get washed once and you're done
You might do it for amusement
I'm parked, I already do it for fun
Counting down to the wire
Just don't let me get to the one

I'm the one
Really...
Too much of me?
Silly...
Three peat

Hope you can afford me?
Five ways to Sunday
I rest on Mondays
It's six degrees of separation
No one going to ignore me
Seven minutes in my heaven
And you'll fall in love with the kid
Ate too much on this piece
Now I feel it's time to go off the grid
Nie, feels like I'm in Poland
Don't let me get to ten
Because I can keep going

PRAYING

Pray
Pray
Pray for him
Stay
Stay
People stay foreign
Wait
Wait
Just wait on it
Pace
Pace
Keep the pace on them
I keep the grace on them
People come in
And switch
Playing games, I got the Nintendo
Come around with the jokes
And I peep the innuendos
Say we cool not complicated
Keep it all simple
They want me to pop
Adolescent face
Like you greased up with pimples
Words cut deep and then you smile in my face
Smirk with the dimples
Tired of the pain
And I'm awaiting on the pleasure
Tired of treating my body like trash
And do more to be a treasure

So, pray for the kid
In 33 years, they can't do what I did
Sometimes I take months off
Had to go off the grid
At times I felt like everything I did was mid
My mind held captive by my thoughts
Had to do a bid
So, pray
Pray
Pray
Pray for him
And to the next man
Just warn him

Summer 2023 taught me so many things and I learned a lot about myself in the span of two months. Mental Health is an ongoing adventure that we must keep working on consistently. From a traumatic experience, I witnessed family and friends rally around me and lift me up to remind me that life is the true blessing. For most of the year, I had focused on living that I put writing on the backburner. Music helped me get through this trying time and reinvigorate me to keep going. We all have a purpose on this earth, and I was able to recapture the meaning of mine. Thank you for reading this collection.

WHAT'S YOUR SECRET?

Paid the cost
So, I could floss
Don't need to say it
I am a boss
No really...
I am a boss
Never bare
I keep the sauce

You all ain't seasoned
How I am
Been doing this for over 20 summers
I been the reason that I can
Switch effortlessly between flows
It's treason to say I can't
The journey
Don't stop believing
In the end

I can't tell you
How to be or how to move
I don't have anything to show
Or need to prove
This helps ease the pain
The pen it soothes
With it, I always win
I cannot lose
I will not
Shall not
I have been

While you have not
Need not
Saying anything cowboy
Don't want to deal with your bebop
You cartoons only on Saturday
My car tunes every time I hip hop
My ass inside my Audi
Only four rings been committed
You ain't up to standard
And I ain't sorry
You keep playing with my mental
And truly you ain't sorry
Yes I'm seasoned and all the bullshit bland
Go get some Lawry's
I been the secret
Best kept and I like to keep it that way
Trying to take my creativity from me
Ain't a dollar going to pay
You think you can attack me?
No, you going to have to pay
I'm prescribed to this shit
Yeah I take it day to day
Under the influence of the pen
Yeah I ain't the one to play

I swear that I'm hardest writer out
No need to classify as a rap
Because when I come with this heat
You had to give your head a scratch
This that finger licking good content
That make you want to slap your mama

And don't let me get carried away
When I see this make some commas
Sorry for the informalities
No need for the extra commas
I just names on all these animals around me
That's why I say cómo te llamas
And that's the only Spanish you get from me
You're retention of the basic language
Is ridiculous to me
Ridiculous
Like I'm watching the MTV show
Because I see all these reruns of my style
Let me syndicate and go
Condolences to you trying
Hell let's send a cake and go
Got to have the secret recipe
And I ain't talking about how to cook
Come talk to me and I'll show you to formulate one of these 12 books

ACKNOWLEDGEMENTS

'Trauma' was inspired by "Cobra", a song from American rapper, Megan Thee Stallion

'Fraud' was inspired by "Fraud", a song from American rapper, Russ

'Circus' was inspired by "Tightrope", a song from American singer, Tinashe

'Unhinged' was inspired by "Demons", a song from American rapper, Doja Cat

'Fuck Everything' was inspired by "FTG", a song from American rapper, Doja Cat

'Oasis' was inspired by "Oasis", a song from American rapper, Russ

'24' was inspired by "24 Hours To Live", a song from American rapper, Joyner Lucas

'Mindless (Uh Huh)' was inspired by "Uh Huh", a song from American singer, Tinashe

'Ramblings (What You Mean)' was inspired by "WYM Freestyle", a song from American rapper, Doja Cat

'Changed' was inspired by "On The Radar Freestyle", a song from American rapper, Ice Spice

'Slimeball' was inspired by "Slime You Out", a song from Canadian rapper, Drake & American singer, SZA

'When We Were Young' was inspired by "When We Were Young", a song from English singer, Adele

'Young & Naive' was inspired by "Used To Be Young", a song from American singer, Miley Cyrus

'A Lot To Be Said' was inspired by "Butterfly Ku", a song from American rapper, Ice Spice

'The Old Me' was inspired by "Nice To Meet You", a song from English singer, Pinkpantheress & English rapper, Central Cee

'Metamorphosis' was inspired by "Balut", a song from American rapper, Doja Cat

'Not Far from Home' was inspired by "Away from Home", a song from Canadian rapper, Drake

'Graveyard' was inspired by "Skull & Bones", a song from American rapper, Doja Cat

'A Morning in Indy' was inspired by "8am in Charlotte", a song from Canadian rapper, Drake

'Raise The Stakes' was inspired by "Raise The Stakes", a song from American rapper, BIA

'Dumb Asses' was inspired by "Shutcho", a song from American rapper, Doja Cat

'Graveyard' was inspired by "Skull & Bones", a song from American rapper, Doja Cat

'Troubled Waters' was inspired by "Virginia Beach", a song from Canadian rapper, Drake

'Fear' was inspired by "Fear of Heights", a song from Canadian rapper, Drake

'I Love It' was inspired by "Love Life", a song from American rapper, Doja Cat

'Glad You Called' was inspired by "Call My Name", a song from American singer, Jordin Sparks

'FPS' was inspired by "First Person Shooter", a song from Canadian rapper, Drake & American rapper J.Cole

'Praying' was inspired by "Pray 4 Da Kiid", a song from American rapper Kriiispy & American rapper, Wxlf

'What's Your Secret' was inspired by "The Secret Recipe", a song from American rapper, Lil Yachty & American rapper, J. Cole

BECAUSE THE INK NEVER DRIES UP

FOLLOW ME ON MY SOCIAL MEDIA

RDJOHNSON.ORG
FACEBOOK: @R.D.JOHNSON
TWITTER: @_RDJOHNSON_
INSTAGRAM: @_RDJOHNSON_